Jill Conner

The Blue Hour

Jill Conner

The Blue Hour

in Max Beckmann's "Large Still-Life with Doves"

PalmArtPress
Berlin

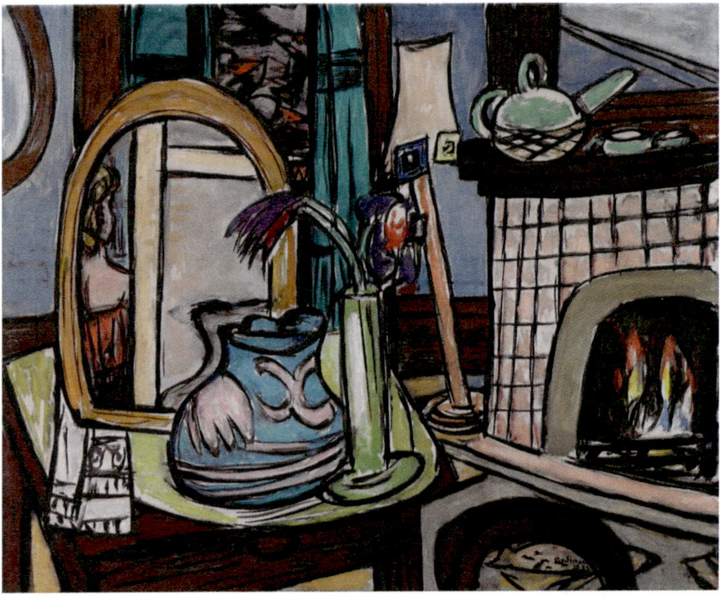

"Large Still-Life with Doves," by Max Beckmann came together in the Autumn of 1950 in New York City. The dark but colorful canvas opens into an empty, blue-walled living room that is furnished with a small, wood table and chair seen near the left-center, with an oversized, white-tiled fireplace on the right. The wood table appears immediately in the foreground and leans toward the viewer, sharing a surface that contains a vase filled with flowers and another with floral decor. While those objects sit in front of a gold-framed mirror, a small fire crackles away just opposite lending a warmth to the green tea service that appears on the mantlepiece above with embers in red, yellow, white and black. The background of the composition consists of a wide, blue wall that extends from each side of the painting. Within this particular area, Beckmann frames the space evenly throughout with a thick, wood trim that divides the painting into three sections, beginning in the lower right corner, before fanning out toward the left in the shape of a half-moon while interweaving a bounty of visual metaphors that extend from left to right.

Two panels of dark green drapes, for instance, punctuate this series of demarcations, and line each side of the window that appears in the background where a small group of gray-white doves are seen roosting together while peering through the framed, glass surface gazing closely upon the interior. The sun has set and the moon is aloft since the darkness of the birds' feathers indicates an iridescent glow. The half-round form of another reflective surface, moreover, appears on the far left, wherein a brush of much lighter white pigment appears to reflect a small section of the candle-lit interior that brings to mind the blue sky and clouds that appear over the East River. A larger glass surface portrayed on the right appears similarly, as a mirror that hangs against the interior wall and reflects the studio's space behind the viewer. Two cables extend diagonally across the surface reflecting the studio's ceiling while also suggesting the cabled supports given to the elevated towers of either the Manhattan or Brooklyn Bridge. The overall viewing experience of "Large Still-Life with Doves" is, therefore, multi-layered while engaging with the unpredictable movement of time. In doing so, the artist presents a circular viewing experience that gradually conveys how significant, personal experiences of the artist have contributed to the progression of Modernism as it expanded from Germany to America.

By September 1950, Max Beckmann was ailing from advanced heart disease and yet he remained overwhelmed by the memorable summer trip that began some months earlier at Washington University in Saint Louis during early June and then concluded during the early part of August in California. In St. Louis, Beckmann received an honorary doctorate and special honors along with Bernard Baruch, Vijaya Lakshimi Pandit and Eugene P. Wigner.[1] In California Beckmann had met Vincent Price, a prominent Hollywood actor who was one of the artist's most enthusiastic collectors. He also reconnected with acquaintances from his early years in Berlin such as Kathi Schaps, William Valentiner, and Marguerite Wildenhain, a Bauhaus ceramicist who had established Pond Farm in 1942 located a few miles north of Oakland in Guerneville, California.

When looking at "Large Still-Life with Doves," the context of the Blue Hour unfolds where one's wishes and desires are embellished by the mind's eye. In this small serendipitous moment that occurs every day before darkness, personal reflections take shape and transform into a combination of symbols and animations. The array of objects and layered perspectives, on view in Max Beckmann's composition, move one back and forth throughout time. While establishing a visual interplay between reflective and flat surfaces, the artist implies specific figures from his past while quietly bringing the viewer into this narrow, but comfortable, living space where mundane details show signs of life.

Berlin

The first viewing trajectory that Max Beckmann employed within "Large Still-Life with Doves," begins with the tip of a chair seen in the foreground, sitting next to the square table that tilts slightly forward toward the viewer. A light green tablecloth covers the surface and is held in place by two vases—one with flowers, the other with flower decor—along with a gold-framed mirror that itself is propped up with a piece of folded newspaper. The reflection in the mirror portrays another feature of the interior, while showing the back of a woman whose blond hair is pinned back and appears in juxtaposition to a form-fitting strapless red dress. This feminine figure also appears to be talking to someone on the other side of the stretched canvas, but that person remains invisible and unknown. The form of the red dress is amplified by the silhouette of a black gown that appears at the opposite edge of the mirror, close to the dulled hue of the gold frame. Even though this figure-suggesting form appears to be a dark reflection of the shorter, light-blue vase that stands on the table in front of the mirror, Max Beckmann suggests otherwise since neither object is an exact replica of the other.

This process of the artist creating personal metaphors while reflecting back on his formative years continues with the folded newspaper seen on the left, where black marks of newsprint vaguely suggest the drawing of a mustached man who wears pince-nez spectacles. Due to the understated placement of these two figures within a structural context that suggests a focus on flowers and ephemera, the identities of both have so far remained unknown. Although the portrait of this individual appears upside down, he seems to wave a salutation while wearing a uniformed cap and coat. However when examining Beckmann's early paintings and drawings made from 1899 to 1913 in connection with the events of his life, the identities of these table-set motifs come within reach. The single, surviving photo-portrait of the Beckmann family from around 1898 shows the young artist standing to the right of his older siblings, Margarethe and Richard, who are both formally dressed. In the sepia-toned photograph, Margarethe sits in a chair on the left wearing a long, white garment with her hair pinned-back while Richard stands tall in a black suit and bow tie at the center of the photo, next to the youthful figure of Max Beckmann.

The Wilhelminian attire worn by both of the siblings became a template for many of Max Beckmann's early artworks that consisted of numerous representations of similarly-dressed men and women who he had encountered in locations such as Ahlshausen, Berlin, Dresden, Hagenring, Leipzig and Magdeburg, while either traveling with his family or attending school. By 1902 when Beckmann purchased a copy of Arthur Schopenhauer's *The World as Will and Representation* (1818), the daily fashion that was required of men and women was formal and became the basis for the artist's

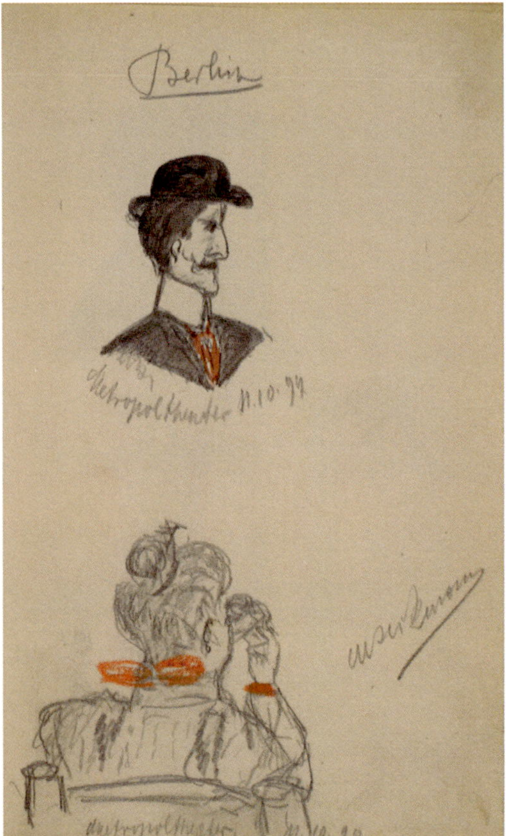
Berlin

exploration of metaphors that highlighted notions of change, progress and regress through an array of male and female interrelationships. Schopenhauer had suggested that the ongoing differences between men and women provided a means through which the individual, or will, could establish a sense of singular identity while existing in juxtaposition to the idea, or society.[2]

Although his siblings receive very little acknowledgment throughout his biography, Margarethe and Richard were highly significant throughout Beckmann's youth. While he made one painting of his sister in 1899, the artist made two drawings of his brother in 1900 that appear in the pages of his first sketchbook. One first sees, for instance, the figure of Richard Beckmann from a slight distance while reclining in a chair and reading. "Zu Hause", or "At Home", was written by the artist in the top margin of the page, followed by "R. Beckmann" below.

In another instance, the artist fills the page with a close-up of his brother's face, including his name in

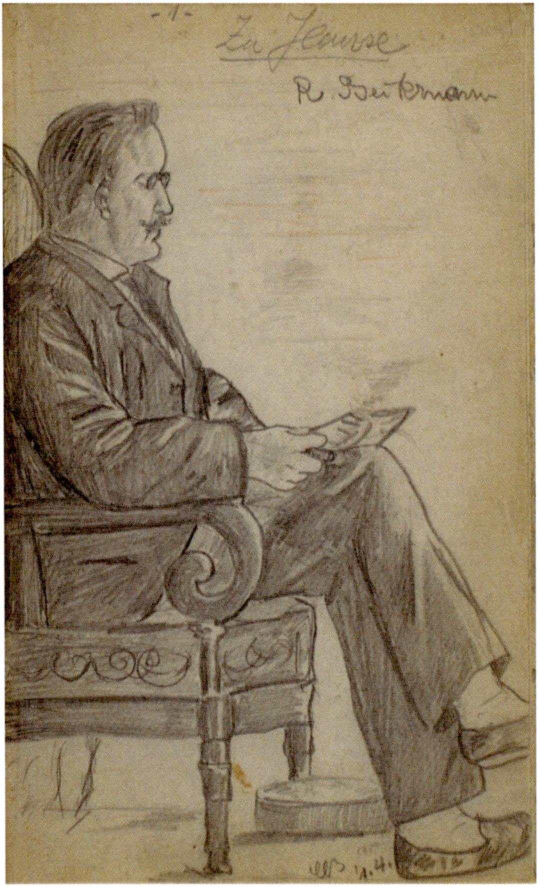
Zu Hause

the margin above while the word "Lesend", or "reading", appears below in red lettering.[3]

In 1895 their father, Carl Beckmann, had died suddenly of a stroke. No visual documentation of him remained. Unlike his older brother, Max Beckmann did not have the chance to collaborate with his father. Richard, however, did have that opportunity and continued to be inspired by the era of invention while the young artist adopted the role of a passive observer who drew his brother's transformation:

> *Max's older brother was similarly devoted to such ideas of being able to discover something. According to the family's scant recollections, this brother must have been interested in discoveries of machines. Compared to Max, he was the favored, admired young man in the family. A typewriter, a hair-drying machine and a washing machine were constructed, but they were never successful. Whenever a machine was almost finished, the product was already available elsewhere. The brother's dream of something new could not be reconciled with the reality of*

his invention … (H)is brother's machine designs were misguided. But they testify to a creative imagination, inspired by the all-pervasive dawn of a new technical age.[4]

In 1899 Richard Beckmann had been registered as a student at the University of Rostock, where he was studying to become a Chemist.[5] He completed his matriculation in 1901, a year before Berlin's U-Bahn opened to the public, and filed his first patent in January 1903 for a device that holds sensitive sheets of paper that create photographic prints.[6] In July, he sailed to New York City for what seems like a short visit, and stayed at the Meyers Hotel in Hoboken, New Jersey.[7] Upon his return to Berlin, Richard Beckmann filed additional patents from his location in Charlottenburg.[8]

In returning to "Large Still-Life with Doves", the transposed portrait of a red-dressed woman initially appears to reference back to an early sketch by Beckmann titled, "Metropoltheater" (October 11, 1899) where a seated woman with coiffed hair is seen from the back while holding a pair of theater glasses for better viewing. This particular motif appears again in the standing figure seen in, "Parade Ground" (March 10, 1900), as an outline above a color drawing titled, "Parade Ground" (March 16, 1900), and in the figure of a woman who is seated alone in a drawing titled "Grüner Jaeger" (March 21, 1900). In each of these instances, Beckmann focuses on the independent, fashionable woman in Wilhelmine, Germany—a figure who was eventually embodied by Minna Tube, Beckmann's primary female model at the start of his career who he first met in 1902 at the Grand Ducal Art Academy in Weimar and with whom he began a long courtship soon after. In 1905, Beckmann painted his first large-scale portrait of Minna that measured approximately 4.5-feet by 2.5-feet. Although they married in 1906, a few months after his mother's death, the artist created a portrait of Minna each year, until he left for World War I, which not only punctuated his

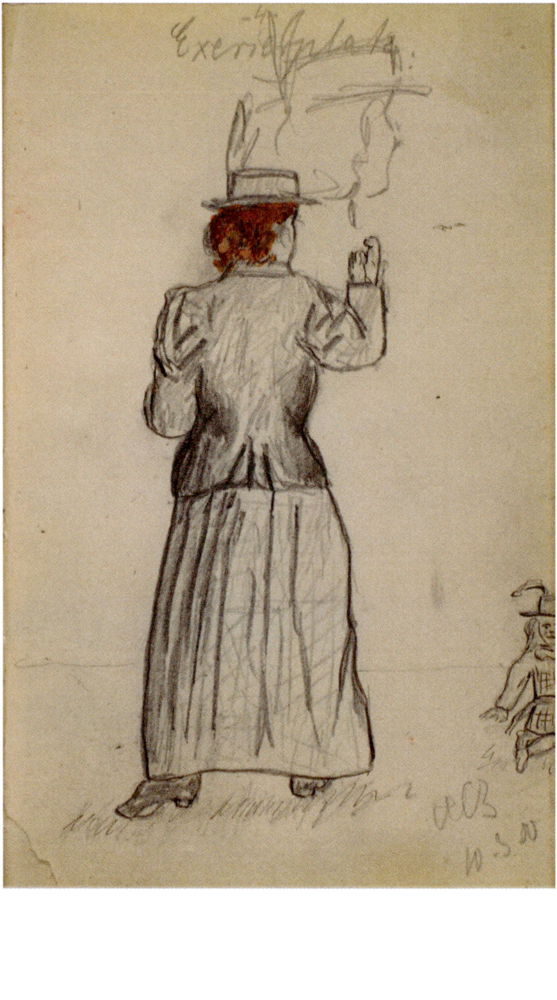

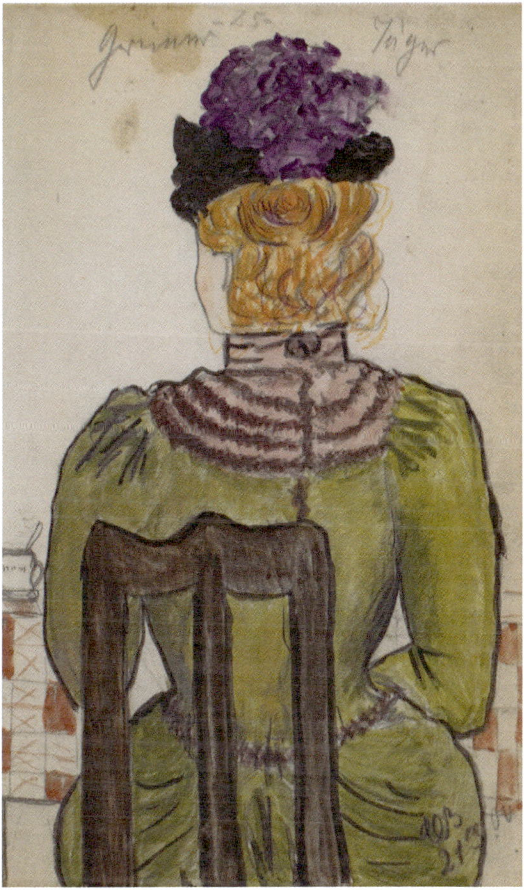

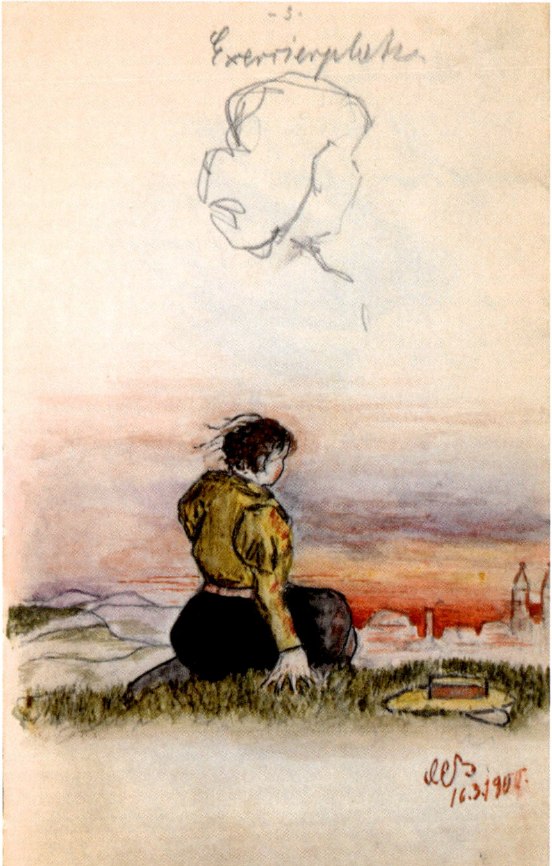

- 3 -
Exerzierplatz
16.3.1905

growing output of paintings but also affirmed that she was indeed his ideal model [9]

1906 was a life-changing year that included an honorary prize from the German Artists Society for "Young Men by the Sea" (1905). The award not only included the acquisition of this painting by the Grand Ducal Museum in Weimar, but it was followed by a residency to the Villa Romana in Florence, Italy. "Young Men by the Sea," was considered a breakthrough within German Modern art at the time due to the way it moved past the oppressive sense of self that was particularly characteristic of the Wilhelmine era since it placed multiple renditions of the traditional male nude figure within the Northern European landscape.

In response to the death of his mother, Beckmann painted "Large Death Scene" (1906) that shows a small family gathering taking place around her, as she passed away. The artist's brushstrokes across this representation are rapid and unsettled. His mother's face also reflects a beast-like representation. Although he combined a sweeping line with dark colors, the intense catharsis appears most prominently in the muscular figure of an unknown man, who sits on the left and leans forward while writhing in grief next to the bedridden, lifeless form while two unknown female figures kneel and stand on the right.

While one could argue that the feminine form seen in "Large Still-Life with Doves" is rather generic when seen in relation to the women who Beckmann drew early on, a similar argument could be made for the representation of his older brother. Beckmann's painting "Large Death Scene" for instance not only confirms the unknown, male figure as the artist's brother, Richard Beckmann, but it also establishes him as the artist's primary male model who posed regularly for the artist's traditional, narrative paintings dating from 1906 to 1913. These similarities, moreover, strongly suggest that Richard and Minna maintained a more prominent role in the artist's life.

One can conclude, therefore, that the two transposed portraits seen in the framed reflection and the folded newspaper within "Large Still-Life with Doves" are Max Beckmann's separate recollections of his first two studio models, whose participation helped him follow his ambition of traditional narrative painting that he had started to pursue prolifically in 1906 after his award from the German Artists' Society. The artist's juxtaposed representation of both figures, moreover, seems to reference two opposing face cards while affirming his perpetual reverence to Richard and Minna, whose burlesque figures tumbled throughout Beckmann's numerous biblical and historical vignettes that brought him increasing acclaim and recognition.

At this time, the city of Berlin continued to transform itself into a modern metropolis that sought to become a symbol of 20th-century urbanism. By 1912, Minna began pursuing a career in singing and was eventually cast in operas that were performed on stages in Elberfeld, Berlin, Wuppertal, Dessau, Chemnitz and Graz.[10] On April 15th, 1912, the Titanic oceanliner collided with an iceberg while crossing the Atlantic Ocean from England to the United States. The catastrophic accident took the lives of at least 1,500 people, many from America's upper class such as John Jacob Astor IV and Benjamin Guggenheim. In April 1913, American Art News published a small paragraph announcing the imminent Berlin debut of Max Beckmann's monumental painting titled, "The Titanic" (1912) that was made in response to this intercontinental calamity: "This artist is already known by his picture exhibited in 1909 of the destruction of Messina."[11]

However after Richard Beckmann emigrated to New York in November of that year, the artist's consistent, venerated rendering of the traditional nude figure as a metaphor within early Modernism suddenly vanished from Beckmann's work, and was replaced by flat, angular forms that were accented with exaggerated gestures and expressions. It can be suggested that this phase of Max Beckmann's career concluded with two paintings titled "Falling Racers" (1913) and "Wrestlers"

(1913).[12] While both compositions portray fraught moments within two different athletic competitions, the contestants appear to face the unbearable challenge of balance, as they work against unwieldy weight and resistance. "Wrestlers," in particular appears to show the artist being pinned down by a figure who looks like his brother.

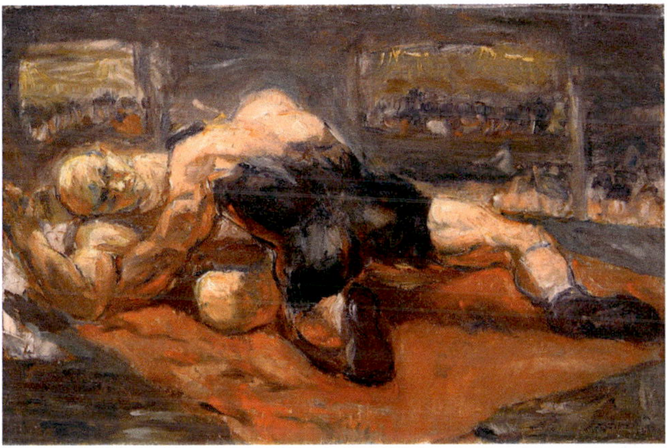

Figures

New York

Upon arriving in New York, Richard identified his closest living relative on the ship's passenger manifest as, "Brother: Herr Max Beckmann, Hermsdorf near Berlin".[13] For the years he spent in New York City, Richard Beckmann first lived as a lodger at 1220 Lexington Avenue, a few doors away from East 86th Street, that was also known as the German Broadway.[14] He had worked as a Chemist for Specialty Manufacturing Co. at 15 Beekman Street near Newspaper Row, followed by Curtis & Knoop and Hall & Ruckel, located between the South Street Seaport and Tribeca, where colors were mixed and healing potions were sealed inside custom-designed, glass bottles. When he died of a stroke in 1926 at Lincoln Hospital, Richard Beckmann had been living near East 165th Street at 969 Cauldwell Avenue in the Bronx, working as a secretary-treasurer for Dermatan Chemical based in Lower Manhattan on Greenwich Street.[15]

Some details of the artist's life from this earlier era can only be deduced from cross-reference since Beckmann's diaries from the 1920s and 1930s were most likely destroyed in May 1940, in compliance with the demands of the Nazi occupation of the Netherlands. Max Beckmann's list of paintings, for instance, not only itemizes a painting titled "Still-Life with Logs" (1926) as an artwork that was dedicated to the memory of his brother, but he also noted that the painting had been included in the debut exhibition that I. B. Neumann had curated in 1927 at his new gallery in Midtown Manhattan, where Neumann had introduced 16 paintings by the artist.[16]

On September 8, 1947 nearly thirty-four years after his brother had permanently moved to America, Max Beckmann disembarked the SS Westerdam with his much younger, second wife Mathilde 'Quappi' Beckmann. Memories of Prewar Berlin returned, a time when the city's urban transformation had ushered in an economic boom before

World War I. Many acquaintances from that era had since immigrated to the United States, and on that September day in 1947 it was Curt Valentin who greeted the new emigrant couple with a bouquet of roses, along with Werner Drewes. Valentin had initially worked as an assistant for the Alfred Flechtheim Gallery and then later for the Karl Buchholtz Gallery—both had represented Beckmann's art in Berlin. Werner Drewes was a former member of the Bauhaus-Dessau who had fled Nazi Germany in 1930 and then later was on faculty at Washington University in St. Louis.

Later that evening, Max and Quappi Beckmann attended a festive, welcome dinner that included the Bauhaus architect Mies van der Rohe and representatives from the Museum of Modern Art. "Well, I'm curious to see if I can endure this wild dream," Beckmann wrote, before leaving to St. Louis nine days later.[17] In that short window of time, Beckmann visited Central Park, the Museum of Modern Art to view his "Departure"-triptych, gave an interview to TIME magazine and made an excursion to the Bronx Zoo. However, before the taxi cab could reach the desired destination located north of Manhattan, Beckmann asked the driver to turn around and drop him off at the Metropolitan Museum of Art, because the Bronx, "I sadly realized was almost in another country."[18] Aside from the fact he had made this excursion alone, Beckmann's written observation carries not only a tone of disappointment but also an unmistakable flair of familiarity.

Even though the context of "Large Still-Life with Doves" is based upon the interior design of Beckmann's last studio located at 38 West 69th Street, the representation also shows itself as the exterior view that the artist had frequently seen in 1949 when walking for extended lengths of time along the East River. The blue walls and wood trim, for instance, suggest the structural silhouette of either the Manhattan Bridge, the Brooklyn Bridge or both. In the first week of September 1949, Beckmann wrote in his journal that he not only ventured East from his new home on 19th Street, but he had also identified the area near the tennis courts along the river near East 10th Street: “In glorious weather, I then discovered a new harbor view to the left [that] can be reached in 25 minutes.”[19]

During the last week of September the artist noted, “Clear and cool was this Jewish New Year’s Day—and I dryly painted the first round for ‘Hercules’ Last Duty’ …Later, a somewhat wistful walk by First Avenue to Lafayette where old bookstores amused me in the cold gloomy evening air.”[20] Beckmann’s walks routinely began with a visit to Stuyvesant Park before extending toward the tip of Manhattan with the city’s elevated railway: “Ventured down to Chinatown on the El. The El to Chatham (Square) was a dreamlike labyrinth, along with Worth Street, Canal Street and back to 7th Avenue over 14th Street.”[21] About a week later, Beckmann took Quappi down to Chinatown to tour her through the area.[22]

In a letter to Minna Beckmann-Tube dated November 25, 1949, the artist detailed his newly-discovered path along the East side of Manhattan that extended from his home on 19th Street up to 96th Street and down to the tip of Manhattan:

> *The narrow 19th is filled with parked cars on the right and left, like almost all streets, and there is only a narrow space for those speeding along. If you walk 4 houses towards the East River, you will find yourself on Second Avenue. A huge street that has constant car traffic of 75-100 miles per hour, which is brilliantly regulated by red and green lights.—As you can see, there is no lack of life and movement in this little town—not to mention the sensations of the 4-5 story subways. I walk 20 minutes to the East River through a huge complex of 15 to 20-story apartment buildings, which from a distance look like backdrops to the Dr. Caligari movie and glow*

> *red at night with millions of windows—I live at the beginning of downtown, which used to be elegant.—It would take me an hour to walk uptown, 20 minutes by subway and 15 minutes by cab—I often drink my coffee there at the Plaza Hotel and then go for a walk in Central Park, which is about 5 times the size of the Tiergarten. In short, there is no lack of variety. As long as your nerves can take it. All in all, NY is of course the ultimate in grotesque gigantism that mankind has achieved so far. It doesn't suit me badly. Ha, ha.*[23]

Lower Manhattan carried a particular allure even when the artist encountered strife along the Bowery: "I live in an all-Italian, Jewish neighborhood and most of the time you only hear 8-10 languages mixed together when you're on the street."[24] Manhattan appeared to be like a much larger version of Berlin.[25]

When Beckmann was not exploring either Lower Manhattan or teaching at the Brooklyn Museum Art School, he made numerous excursions over to Irving Place and then around Gramercy Park to Lexington Avenue. Within a few weeks, Lexington was Beckmann's primary route when traveling uptown. The Longchamps restaurant was one of Beckmann's most preferred to visit with Quappi, where they often dined among the murals of Winold Reiss, that were located at the Chanin Building on 42nd Street, and at two locations on 57th Street near the Buchholtz Gallery and I.B. Neumann's New Art Circle Gallery—the two representatives of Max Beckmann's art in New York.[26]

On other evenings Beckmann could be found ordering dinner with Louise and Maurice Freedman at the Chateaubriand on East 56th Street, that was most likely followed by drinks at Freeman Chum's on East 53rd Street. At this time the Chateaubriand was the primary destination for French cuisine while Freeman Chum's was known for its late-night atmosphere that was heavy with nostalgia.[27] The Hans Jäger Restaurant, located at 1253 Lexington Avenue near 85th Street, hosted the artist at least twice. Otherwise, Beckmann also basked in the ambiance at either The Plaza, The St. Regis, The Gladstone and The Ritz-Carlton—all located between 46th and 59th Streets near Lexington Avenue.[28] While most of these restaurants and their locations at that time are no longer in business, the interior view of the artist's apartment as portrayed in "Large Still-Life with Doves" along with the base of the Manhattan Bridge, as suggested by the white-tiled fireplace, still exists.

Toward the right side of the painting, a free-standing floor lamp appears in the back corner of the room, followed by a green teapot, with two coordinating cups, that are set upon the mantle above the fireplace. One could say that the tall vase of wilted flowers either refers to the artist's idea of his older self or serves as a motif from the field of naturalism, alluding to the memories of his early years in

Braunschweig, where fields were abundant and the identification of various trees and flowers were part of a hobby that occurred while on walks with his father.[29] The blue and yellow square pendants attached to the white lamp shade, therefore, suggest the flag colors of the Duchy of Braunschweig from 1830 to 1918, when it was an autonomous part of the Confederation of the Rhine and later the German Empire.

As seen throughout this painting, the artist battled his recollections conjured by what he saw before him: "A long melancholic walk in the rain on the East River to Canal Street. Everything was wrapped in a thick fog, like my soul. Took the El back. At times I was so confused in the Bowery that I felt very distressed. Finally home all soaked and tired."[30] In early October, Beckmann took the El to the Bronx and disembarked at the station on East 165th Street. While he made no mention of his brother in his diary, he was only two blocks away from Richard's last residence on Cauldwell Avenue.

However Beckmann did note in his journal that he had discovered a racetrack and had been able to see the tall buildings of Rockefeller Plaza in the distance.[31]

St. Louis, Los Angeles and Oakland

While the green tea service seen on the mantle above the fireplace appears oddly funerary, it is actually an appropriation of a Bauhaus ceramic style that had been designed by Marguerite Wildenhain (neeé Friedländer) in the 1920s. However, as the fire gradually burns away in the dark enclave below, these three vessels became symbolic of the weeks that Beckmann spent on the West Coast, where a prewar community of German exiles continued to create and appeal to new audiences in America. Max and Quappi Beckmann were on their way to join this coterie when they left the hustle of New York City on June 2nd, 1950. It was also the evening when the Brooklyn Dodgers broke their short losing streak with a win against the St. Louis Cardinals in Missouri.[32]

As the train was first bound for St. Louis, the artist began his own odyssey through the clouds of memory. Life in New York had not been without challenges, and while the train continued to stretch north past Albany, Beckmann surmised, "I don't know—at least I don't dislike the city."[33] When darkness covered the sky, he added, "I now continue to dream."[34] Soon after, Beckmann received an honorary degree on Tuesday, June 6th from Washington University in St. Louis. In a lecture given to the Friends and Faculty of Philosophy at the University, Beckmann stated:

> *Time goes by fast like a dream, and I am very thankful for all the love and support of loyal friends who made the first phase of my immigration beautiful and light.—You cannot fathom what an inner upheaval it was for me to come to this peaceful country after the terrible destruction I had to witness in Europe. For this reason, and many others, the time in St. Louis will always remain unforgettable to me.*[35]

This was followed by a packed commencement ceremony where Dean Hudson had introduced Max Beckmann to an audience of 6,500 people as Chancellor Compton bestowed the honorary doctorate degree.[36]

By Thursday night, the Beckmanns were already relaxing in the roomette of a cross-country train that was destined for Los Angeles, California. The route first traveled south across Kansas, before turning northward into the approaching night. "The most beautiful thing was El Paso," Beckmann wrote, "over whose grotesque cliffs and rocks you can see Mexico, and where the Rio Grande met us. Later one also saw the Cross of El Paso," most likely referring to Mt. Cristo Reyes.[37] When they arrived in Los Angeles, the Beckmanns were met by William Valentiner, who drove them to a garden party that was taking place at the home of Vincent Price, where guests socialized and mingled among exotic foliage and sculptures from the South seas.

Valentiner was a familiar face from 1905, when he was the Director of the Kaiser Friedrich Museum and the Kunstgewerbemuseum in Berlin.[38] Beckmann's reacquaintance with Valentiner was a perfect antecedent to their next destination in Monterey. A few hours later, after a drive through Hollywood, Max and Quappi were back on a commuter train traveling to Carmel-by-the-Sea. Upon their arrival in San Francisco, they transferred to a taxi that drove along the curvilinear coastline and passed by Half Moon Bay as their view from the car provided sweeping ocean views.

Although dead-tired despite an early arrival, the Beckmanns were thrilled to finally meet their host, Kathi Schaps, who had been a well-known figure in Berlin's soirée society. George Mosson, a prominent member of the Berlin Secession, had painted a portrait of Schaps that was reproduced in the 1926/1927 volume of Velhagen & Klasings Monatshefte, next to an article by Dr. Wolfgang Bruhn titled, "Women's Dress in Fashion and

Painting over Two Centuries," that was an essay written in response to an exhibition at the Kunstgewerbemuseum.[39] Beckmann brought all of these disparate details together in a letter to Minna stating, "Our host finally turned out to be from Berlin's Jewish upper crust, an emigrée from the Liebermann and Cassirer circles."[40] For the following evening, Schaps had cooked a chicken for dinner and they spoke of old times.

Afterward, "I was allowed to rest under a lousy portrait of a lady on horseback, a still-life by 'Mosson' from the Berlin Secession, and a beer garden scene by Liebermann—gently lulled by the thunder of the Pacific and the barking of dogs."[41] In her memories of Max Beckmann, Minna also included some details of their dinner parties in Berlin during those early years, that had included Paul Cassirer, Max Lieberman, Georges Mosson, Frank Wedekind, Max Reinhardt, Alexander Moss, Tilla Durieux, Konrad von Kordoff, Walther Rathenau, Rainer Maria Rilke and Hugo von Hofmannsthal.[42]

After Max Beckmann's first walk to the ocean swamps and expansive sand dunes—where he watched two large birds circle the wetlands for food—his longing for the past led him to connect it with the world before him.[43] He explained to Minna, "It's also really quite wide, and the Pacific is a great barrier with the Marquis and Easter Islands to the left, and Japan and India to the right. Finally a little further, and you're in Iraq, then Italy and an alligator's leap to Munich."[44] Carmel, for that matter, was a version of the Black Forest with the Pacific Ocean as an added feature.[45]

Once he began teaching at Mills College in July, Henry Schaeffer-Simmern stopped by Beckmann's studio for a visit and to see the artist's solo show at the Mills College art gallery. The paintings on view were mostly from the private collection of Sigmund Morgenroth and his son, Stephan Lackner (born Ernst Gustave Morgenroth) who had known Beckmann during the 1920s when he was teaching in Frankfurt.[46] The subjects of the paintings were mostly landscapes and seascapes that portrayed different locations throughout France and Germany.[47]

From an interview with the San Francisco Chronicle: "Beckmann let fall only one comment during our tour: 'I only make simple pictures.' Period. Perhaps, however, there is a little more to it than that."[48] More importantly, Beckmann disclosed that since his move to America he had discovered the paintings of George Catlin, an American anthropologist from the 19th-century who had painted indigenous peoples of North America and the surrounding Western landscapes.[49] However, due to the fact that his drawings were classified as part of anthropology, Catlin's art had been stored away from public view.[50]

Although Beckmann does not directly mention Marguerite Wildenhain in his journal from 1950, he wrote about an excursion that he took from Oakland to a pottery school on August 3rd: "In the evening we went to the ceramics school with all types of guys and a lot of meatloaf. But it was quite funny with the pot people, even a Greek painter was there." While Beckmann was certainly referring to the Pond Farm ceramics colony located in Guerneville, he was also most likely referring to Jean Varda, a painter who had lived in California and was a very active member at Pond Farm during its early years.

Memory Palace

If one considers "Large Still-Life with Doves" as a private repository that condenses different remnants of the artist's personal memories, time is not only the essence of this painting but these everyday objects, initially mundane and void of meaning, become motifs with connotations that highlight Max Beckmann's associations with specific individuals, events and moments that appeared during his early years in Berlin (1904-1914). This symbolism, construed over time, brings the viewer back to the beginning of the painting, where one stands in front and looks to the center. By sharing the standpoint of the painter, the observer gazes across the room, past the vignettes of still-life arrangements, and sees three gray doves in the background.

As birds, their heads quickly dart back and forth while looking. However, Beckmann's painting catches them in a stop-motion moment. The zig-zag shape of thick, black lines that frame the birds references back to the late 1920s when social unrest spread rapidly throughout Germany. This was underscored by further acts of violence that the Nazis had sanctioned while their political power increased. In 1930, Beckmann read *Ulysses* (1920) by James Joyce, an epic tale set in 1904 Dublin, Ireland that is a cynical account of one day in the life of Leopold Bloom, a man of Irish and Jewish decent.

In his copy of the book, Beckmann had underlined: "Beware of what you wish for in youth because you will get it in the middle of life."[51] Within the short time-span of 24 hours, Bloom experiences the realities of infidelity, loss, fantasy and racism—crushing characteristics of the modern world. "Belief in himself," wrote Joyce, "has been untimely killed. He was overborne in a cornfield first (a ryefield, I should say) and he will never be a victor in his own eyes after nor play victoriously the game of laugh and lie down. Assumed dongiovanism will not save him."[52] The narrative presents an unlimited number of characters and collates rapid gestures with truncated, colloquial English. Although Beckmann read the text in German, several passages of Joyce's narrative, such as these, resonated.

Birds, moreover, did not become a primary subject in Beckmann's paintings until 1938, after he had been fired from his teaching position in Frankfurt and labelled a degenerate artist by the German government. "Hell of the Birds," (1938) is the artist's first painting that focuses on this subject, and shows a crowded, savage scene of figures that appear similar to the ethnographic drawings of Hopi Katchina. Beckmann's busy scene shows several bird-like personalities acting out a ritual of human sacrifice. In "Warrior and Siren," (1939) Beckmann suggests a scene from Homer's *Odyssey* where Odysseus pauses and listens to a deceitful temptress. Four rather bland paintings titled "The Seagulls" (1940), "Brown Ocean with Seagulls" (1941), "Seagulls in the Storm" (1942) and "Sunning Seagulls" (1942), show several birds with gray-and-white feathers that appear along a generic ocean shore while looking toward the viewer, who is engaged in looking past them, toward the horizon line that appears at the ocean's edge.

However in Beckmann's "Large Still-Life with Doves," the birds placed along the painting's horizon line are shown to peer through the glass window indicating that they are seeking sustenance as well as a gain of access to the apartment's interior. In *Episode 12* of *Ulysses*, Joyce's narrative ventures into a stuffy Irish pub and employs the frequent sound and subject of the word "I" with the intention of juxtaposing one's personal vision with other world views. Similar to the large, overarching toucans seen in Beckmann's "Begin the Beguin," (1946) where tall, domineering figures are defined by the awkward, physical disabilities of two dancers, the three gray doves pry remotely at their subject, each with one eye, and perform similarly to James Joyce's anti-Semitic citizen, whose lower case name consists of two "i"s while maintaining only one point of view: "There's no one as blind as the fellow that won't see, if you know what I mean."[53] Like the citizen, the birds observe from a distance while watching the asymmetry of daily life attempt to correct itself.

Like Joyce, Beckmann presents a personal vision that is seen in juxtaposition: "Force, hatred, history, all that. That's not life for men and women, insult and hatred. And everybody knows that it's the very opposite of that that is really life."[54] The doves, therefore, are not symbols of peace as one would first think, but rather they stand as symbols of the artist's ongoing memories of having lived through Nazi-occupied Amsterdam, with its ongoing violence and invasiveness. Similar to Joyce, Beckmann presents multiple scenes within one framework that show themselves as metaphors of life-changing events such as infidelity, loss, fantasy and racism that occurs not only over the course of each day but also over time.

By the end of the Summer of 1950, Max and Quappi Beckmann had traveled to at least eight cities within two months. In late August, the artist made a visit to Stuyvesant Park. He was walking around Lexington and Fifth Avenue on September 2nd, when a new cover of *The New Yorker* appeared on the news stands and featured a drawing by Leonard Dove. Dove's depiction portrays a landscape vista with a man wearing a white summer suit and hat while walking away into the background on the left. Beckmann had been known for taking long walks and wearing white linen clothes during summer months. This figure drawn by Dove is shown in a surrealistic context where the wide asphalt of an airport runway doubles as either an empty road or parking lot. The small fleet of automobiles, seen in the far-off distance, contributes to the drawing's ambiguity. With his back to the paved Exit sign seen in the foreground, a small group of two women and children appear directly opposite, within a small corner on the right, showing expressions of exhaustion as they appear to dwell in the sweltering heat. While one could suggest a similarity between Max

Beckmann and the unknown male figure seen on *The New Yorker's* cover, no one knows for sure if this figure was intended to be Max Beckmann.

On September 23, Beckmann had almost made a successful trip to the Bronx, but not quite. At that time, the artist and his wife were living on West 69th Street near Central Park far away from the Third Avenue El. By the time he began working on "Large Still-Life with Doves" a short time later, the artist was pleased that "Hell of the Birds," had just been exhibited in the Faculty Show at the Brooklyn Museum. Beckmann continued to remain focused on the still-life, dove painting for the next four weeks. A few days before finishing the composition on October 24th, Beckmann had finally reached the Bronx Zoo where he saw a condor, giraffes and kangaroos.[55]

While mundane in recollection, this short trip was significant since at this time Beckmann was too frail to take the train, and he had attempted this same excursion a few years earlier but was then too new to New York to understand the chasm of appearances that existed between Manhattan, Morrisania and other parts of the Bronx. For Max Beckmann, the notion of home was a multi-dimensional location that existed simultaneously within his memories of the past and his perception of the present. Curt Valentin stopped by the studio on November 19th to pick up the painting and formally acquired it on December 11th. "Large Still-Life with Doves" was one of the artist's last still-life paintings completed before he died on December 27, 1950. It was purchased five years later by Morton May, and in 1970 it entered the permanent collection of the Bavarian State Painting Collections.

Afterword

A few years ago, I took a bus across the FDR Drive while commuting to Midtown Manhattan and experienced a feeling of dejá-vù as the bus approached the base of the Manhattan Bridge. In this moment tall, brick apartment buildings towered above an empty sports field next to the gray, stone-masoned base of the bridge. This unique urban perspective created an unresolved association and led to several more trips in this direction until I realized that my mind was associating this specific, mundane scene with the enclosed space that was portrayed by Max Beckmann in his painting titled, "Large Still-Life with Doves" from October 1950.

Max Beckmann has been one of the most interesting subjects to emerge in the Modern era since his legacy has left so much unsaid even though he lived through two world wars and traveled extensively. Much of the collective memory about his life in the

United States has survived primarily in the form of anecdotes. As a result, no significant impression of who Beckmann really was has ever materialized. Despite the fact that a large number of his paintings are located in museums nationwide, Beckmann's legacy is very faint despite the fact that the last three years of his life, from 1947 to 1950, were strikingly the most memorable for himself and the American public.

In January 1948, for instance, the artist noted in his diary that he and his wife Mathilde "Quappi" Beckmann had taken a train from St. Louis to Chicago for a short trip. Although the weather had been very cold, the Beckmanns dined that evening with Mies van der Rohe and, soon following, had an afternoon tea with Peter Selz the following day.[56] Despite the fact that Selz's recollection of this event was off by a year, Beckmann had asked Selz about his experience of teaching at The New Bauhaus, a school that had been founded in Chicago by Laszlo and Sibylle Moholy-Nagy in 1937.

Within five days of their arrival, Max and Quappi returned to St. Louis and in 1949 the curriculum of The New Bauhaus had been absorbed into the Illinois Institute of Technology by Mies van der Rohe, who had been the Dean of Architecture at that time. Likewise, Max Beckmann received a new teaching position at the Brooklyn Museum Art School that began later that Fall.

According to the enrollment records of the Brooklyn Museum Art School, the student population increased significantly during Max Beckmann's brief tenure. In the Spring of 1949 prior to the artist's arrival, the total student population was 1,009. At the time Beckmann began teaching, the population increased to 1,314; to 1,549 in the Spring of 1950 and to 1,509 in the Fall of 1950.[57] Although most of the students in New York did not provide very substantial recollections, those from California did. Nathan Oliveira, for instance, considered Beckmann as, "a very fundamental man, whose only interest was painting—that's all he wanted to do. Still, I think from our encounters he communicated, indirectly, what artistic values were about," while Robert S. Neumann said, "just the aura of having him standing and looking at your painting was very interesting. He made his feelings felt some way, just by looking at him you could get the idea of what he felt."[58] Students viewed Max Beckmann as a charismatic teacher who bridged painting of the Modern era with the larger picture of European tradition.[59]

When Quappi described the homesickness she felt while living on East 19th Street, she suggested that Beckmann's acceptance of their new life in New York was easier since he seemed to accept it as a new point of view.[60] I was interested in the fact that Beckmann indicated he had been to New York once before, although he had not. His excursions throughout the city, moreover, were extensive. After relocating from the Gramercy District to 69th Street on the Upper West Side in September 1950 one can easily consider "Large Still-Life with Doves," as a memorial to his daily life. On the East Side of Manhattan his long walks evoked the memories of his brother, his early years as an artist in Berlin, along with associations that had been connected to the German immigrant communities located within the New York City neighborhoods of Morrisania, Yorkville, the East Village, the Lower East Side, the Seaport and the area of Lower Manhattan now known as TriBeCa. Max Beckmann's distant experience of New York began in 1927, three years before the Museum of Modern Art opened, and again in the decade before the opening of Lincoln Center. One could suggest that when Max Beckmann set foot on U.S. soil in September 1947, remnants of New York City's multi-layered history came to life: the Progressive Era (1896-1917), the Jazz Age (1918-1929) and the Roaring Twenties (1920-1929).

I have long been interested in the recontextualization of Germany's Weimar Republic (1919-1933) after it splintered across the United States during the late 1930s, when prominent cultural figures from

Germany sought refuge in the United States from Nazi persecution. The close-knit, collaborative character of the Bauhaus, for instance, was divided across a large population of American students who had approached such a significant moment with light curiosity. By the end of the war, the remnants of prewar German culture had saturated into the large geography of the United States.

Endnotes

1"2201 Washington U. Graduates Receive Degrees, Hear Baruch on Ways to Meet Communist Threat; Honorary Awards Presented to Elder Statesman and Five Others at 89th Commencement Exercises in Field House - 2000 Extra Seats Placed on Lawn," *St. Louis Post-Dispatch*, Tuesday, June 6, 1950, page 3. The newspaper article identifies Bernard Baruch as a statesman for the United States who had advised Presidents. The five other honorary degrees were bestowed to, "Eugene P. Wigner, atomic physicist and Princeton University professor, doctor of science. Mrs. Vijaya Lakshmi Pandit, Indian Ambassador to the United States, doctor of laws. Luther Ely Smith, attorney, doctor of laws. Alexander S. Langsdorf, dean emeritus, Washington University School of Engineering, doctor of science. Max Beckmann, artist, doctor of fine arts."

2 Arthur Schopenhauer, The World As Will and Idea (Everyman Library, 1995).

3 Max Beckmann, *Die Skizzenbücher / The Sketchbooks* (Hatje Cantz, 2010).

4 Peter Beckmann, *Max Beckmann: Leben und Werk* (Belser Verlag, 1982), 11-12.

5 "Matrikelportral Rostock ab 1419," Universität Rostock, http://matrikel.uni-rostock.de/.

6 United States Patent Office. Official Gazette of the United States Patent Office. (Washington D.C.) Volume 106, October 13, 1903; 1694. United States Patent Office. Official Gazette of the United States Patent Office. (Washington D.C.) Volume 129, August 20,1907; 3026. Kaiserlich Patentamt. Auszüge aus den Patentschriften. Volume 30, Juli 1909. (Berlin: Carl Heyman Verlag) 1748-49.

7 United States Citizenship and Immigration Services, List or Manifest of Alien Passengers for the U.S. Immigration Officer at Port of Arrival for the S.S. Barbarossa from Bremen on July 18th to

New York on July 29th, 1903 (The Statue of Liberty & Ellis Island),
8 Ibid., United States Patent Office.
9 Stephan Reimertz. *Eine Liebe im Porträt* (Rohwolt Taschenbuch Verlag, 2002), 82.
10 Susanne Petri and Hans-Werner Schmidt, *Max Beckmann: Von Angesicht zu Angesicht* (Hatje Cantz, 2011) 240.
11 "A 'Titanic' Picture," *American Art News*, April 5, 1913. Vol. XI, No. 25, 1.
12 "Falling Racer" in a private collection in NYC - Staatsgalerie Stuttgart took the photograph "Wrestler" is in the collection of the Museum Pfalzgalerie Kaiserslautern. Foto: Gunther Balzer
13 United States Immigration Services. U.S. Immigration Officer at Port of Arrival for the S.S. Pennsylvania Sailing from Hamburg-Cuxhaven, November 8th, 1913 to New York on November 21, 1913, https://www.ancestry.com/discoveryui-content/view/ 4014553633:7488 .
14 Helen Worden, Discover New York with Helen Worden (American Women's Voluntary Services, Inc., 1943), 105.
15 United States City Directories 1822-1925, New York, New York City 1915-1925.
16 Max Beckmann, *Heft 1: Bilder von 1904-1934 in Berlin, Frankfurt, Paris und wieder Berlin.* List of Paintings 1925-1926, Smithsonian Archives of American Art, Unpublished.
17 Max Beckmann, *Tagebücher 1940-1950*, September 10, 1947 (A. Langer - G. Müller, 1955) 208.
18 Ibid., September 13, 1947, 209.
19 Ibid., September 19, 1949, 338.
20 Ibid., September 24, 1949, 339-340.
21 Ibid., September 23, 1949, 339.
22 Ibid., September 30, 1949, 341.
23 Max Beckmann, Briefe III (Piper, c. 1993-1996), 293-294.
24 Ibid., 280.
25 Ibid., 297.

26 *Tagebücher 1940-1950*, 345, 358.
27 Madeline Gray and Vass De Lo Padua, *How To Be A Success in the Restaurant Business* (Greenberg Publisher, 1946), 224.
28 Ibid., 344-45; 346; 348; 349; 353.
29 Max Beckmann, Briefe I (Piper, c. 1993-1996), 197-198.
30 *Tagebücher 1940-1950*, September 29, 1949, 341.
31 Ibid., October 9, 1949, 343.
32 Martin J. Haley, "Bums Bounce Back In Rain to Clip Birds, 8-1," St. Louis Globe-Democrat, June 3, 1950, 36.
33 Ibid., June 2, 1950, 375.
34 Ibid.
35 Max Beckmann, *Die Realität der Träume in den Bildern: Schriften und Gespräche 1911 bis 1950* (Piper, 1990), 73.
36 "2201 Washington U. Graduates Receive Degrees, Hear Baruch on Ways to Meet Communist Threat; Honorary Awards Presented to Elder Statesman and Five Others at 89th Commencement Exercises in Field House - 2000 Extra Seats Placed on Lawn," St. Louis Post-Dispatch, Tuesday, June 6, 1950, page 3. "Communism Is Criminal, Baruch Says at W.U.," St. Louis Globe Democrat, Wednesday, June 7, 1950, page 2.
37 *Tagebücher 1940-1950*, June 9, 1950, 377.
38 *Max Beckmann: Von Angesicht zu Angesicht*, 332.
39 Dr. Wolfgang Bruhn, "Die Frauenkleid in Mode und Malerei Seit Zweijahrhunderten," Velhagen & Klasings Monatshefte. 41 Jahrgang, 1926-1927. 1 Band, 448.
40 *Briefe III*, 325.
41 Ibid., 325-326.
42 Minna Beckmann-Tube, "Erinnerungen an Max Beckmann," in *Frühe Tagebücher 1903/1904 & 1912/1913* (Piper Verlag, 1985), 174-176.
43 *Tagebücher 1940-1950*, June 13, 1950, 378.

44 *Briefe III*, 325.
45 Ibid.
46 "Stephan Lackner," Arts in Exil - Virtual Museum, https://kuenste-im-exil.de/KIE/Content/EN/SpecialExhibitions/MaxBeckmann-en/Persons/01ThePreExileYears/lackner-stephan-en.html.
47 Alfred Frankenstein, "Two Artists and Several Galleries," San Fransisco Chronicle, August 6, 1950, 20.
48 Ibid.
49 Ibid.
50 Ibid.
51 James Joyce, Ulysses (First Vintage Books Edition, June 1986). p. 161. Peter Beckmann, Die Bibiliothek Max Beckmanns. Worms am Rhein: Wernersche Verlagsgesellschaft mbH. 1992, 423.
52 Peter Beckmann, 423.
53 James Joyce, 267.
54 Ibid., 273.
55 *Tagebücher 1940-1950*, October 24, 1950, 394.
56 Paul J. Karlstrom, Peter Selz: Sketches of a Life in Art. (University of California Press, 2012).
57 Records of the Brooklyn Museum Art School: Departmental administration. Course descriptions [01] (1948-1974).
58 Cynthia Haven, Stanford Report, "Stanford's acclaimed artists, Nathan Oliveira, dies at 81," November 17, 2010. Archives of American Art. Oral history interview with Robert S. Neuman, May 1 – June 19, 1991. (Washington, D.C.: Smithsonian, 1991).
59 Ibid., Haven.
60 Mathilde Quappi Beckmann, Mein Leben mit Max Beckmann (Piper Verlag, 1985), 86.

Bibliography

1. American Art News, April 5, 1913. Vol. XI, No. 25
2. Archives of American Art. Oral history interview with Robert S. Neuman, May 1 – June 19, 1991. Washington D.C.: Smithsonian, 1991.
3. Arts in Exil - Virtual Museum, https://kuenste-im-exil.de/KIE/Content/EN/SpecialExhibitions/MaxBeckmann-en/Persons/01ThePreExileYears/lackner-stephan-en.html .
4. Beckmann, Mathilde. Mein Leben mit Max Beckmann. München: Piper Verlag, 1985.
5. Beckmann, Max. Briefe Band I 1899-1925. München: Piper Verlag, 1993.
6. Beckmann, Max. Briefe Band III 1937-1950. München: Piper Verlag, 1996.
7. Beckmann, Max. Die Realität der Träume in den Bildern: Schriften und Gespräche 1911 bis 1950. München: Piper Verlag, 1990.
8. Beckmann, Max. Frühe Tagebücher 1903/04 1912/13. München: Piper Verlag, 1985
9. Beckmann, Max. Heft 1: Bilder von 1904-1934 in Berlin, Frankfurt, Paris und wieder Berlin List of Paintings 1925-1926. Washington D.C.: Smithsonian Archives of American Art, Unpublished.
10. Beckmann, Max. Tagebücher 1940-1950. München: Langen-Müller, 1955.
11. Beckmann-Tube, Minna. "Erinnerungen an Max Beckmann," in Frühe Tagebücher, 1903/04 1912/13. München: Piper Verlag, 1985.
12. Beckmann, Peter. Die Bibliothek Max Beckmanns. Worms am Rhein: Wernersche Verlagsgesellschaft mbH, 1992.
13. Beckmann, Peter. Max Beckmann Leben und Werk. Zurich: Belser Verlag, 1982.
14. Brooklyn Art Museum. Records of the Brooklyn Museum Art School: Departmental administration. Course descriptions [01] (1948-1974).

15. Brooklyn Art Museum. Records of the Brooklyn Museum Art School: Departmental administration. Enrollment [01] (1955-67).
16. Bruhn, Wolfgang. “Die Frauenkleid in Mode und Malerei Seit Zweijahrhunderten,” Velhagen & Klasings Monatshefte. 41 Jahrgang, 1926-1927. 1 Band, 448.
17. Frankenstein, Alfred. “Two Artists and Several Galleries,” San Fransisco Chronicle, August 6, 1950.
18. Joyce, James. Ulysses. Edited by Hans Walter Gabler. New York: Vintage, 1986.
19. Gray, Madeleine and De Lo Padua, Vass. How To Be A Success in the Restaurant Business. Greenberg Publisher, 1946.
20. Haley, Martin J. “Bums Bounce Back In Rain to Clip Birds, 8-1,” St. Louis Globe-Democrat, June 3, 1950.
21. Haven, Cynthia. Stanford Report, “Stanford’s acclaimed artists, Nathan Oliveira, dies at 81,” November 17, 2010.
22. Kaiserlich Patentamt. Auszüge aus den Patentschriften. Volume 30. Berlin: Carl Heyman Verlag, Juli 1909.
23. Karlstrom, Paul J. Peter Selz: Sketches of a Life in Art. Berkeley: University of California Press, 2012.
24. Max Beckmann und J. B. Neumann: Der Künstler und sein Händler in Briefen und Dokumenten 1917 – 1950. Edited by Ursula Harter and Stephan von Wiese. Köln: Verlag der Buchhandlung Walther König, 2011.
25. Max Beckmann: Von Angesicht zu Angesicht. Ostfildern: Hatje Cantz Verlag, 2011.
26. Reimertz, Stephan. Ein Liebe im Porträt. Hamburg: Rowohlt Taschenbuch Verlag. 2002.
27. Schopenhauer, Arthur. The World As Will and Idea. Everyman Library, 1995.
28. St. Louis Post-Dispatch, Tuesday, June 6, 1950, page 3: “2201 Washington U. Graduates Receive Degrees, Hear Baruch on Ways to

Meet Communist Threat; Honorary Awards Presented to Elder Statesman and Five Others at 89th Commencement Exercises in Field House - 2000 Extra Seats Placed on Lawn."
29. U.S. Directories. New York, New York, 1899-1955. New York Public Library.
30. United States Citizenship and Immigration Services, List or Manifest of Alien Passengers for the U.S. Immigration Officer at Port of Arrival for the S.S. Barbarossa from Bremen on July 18th to New York on July 29th, 1903 (The Statue of Liberty & Ellis Island), https://heritage.statueofliberty.org .
31. United States City Directories 1822-1925, New York, New York City 1915-1925. New York Public Library.
32. United States Immigration Services. U.S. Immigration Officer at Port of Arrival for the S.S. Pennsylvania Sailing from Hamburg-Cuxhaven, November 8th, 1913 to New York on November 21, 1913, https://www.ancestry.com/discoveryui-content/view/4014553633:7488 .
33. United States Patent Office. Official Gazette of the United States Patent Office. Volume 106. (Washington D.C.) October 13, 1903.
34. United States Patent Office. Official Gazette of the United States Patent Office. Volume 129. (Washington D.C.) August 20,1907.
35. Worden, Helen. Discover New York with Helen Worden. American Women's Voluntary Services, Inc. 1943.

First Edition 2026, PalmArtPress, Berlin

ISBN: 978-3-96258-235-7

German Edition:
Die Blaue Stunde – in „Max Beckmanns Großes Stilleben mit Tauben“
ISBN: 978-3-96258-241-8

Cover “Large Still-Life with Doves”, 1950
© Photo: Sibylle Forster, Bayerische Staatsgemäldesammlungen.
Bayerische Staatsgemäldesammlungen
Sammlung Moderne Kunst in der Pinakothek der Moderne München.

Layout: NicelyMedia
Printed in Europe

PalmArtPress
Publisher: Catharine J. Nicely
Pfalzburgerstr. 69, 10719 Berlin
www.palmartpress.com

Selected books from PalmArtPress

Martina J. Kohl
FAMILY MATTERS – *Of Life in Two Worlds*
ISBN: 978-3-96258-143-5
244 Pages, Novel, Softcover/Flaps, English

Kevin McAleer
L.A. KID
ISBN: 978-3-96258-193-0
316 Pages, Novel, Softcover/Flaps, English

Dennis McCort
The Golden Pot – *A Fairytale for Our Time*
ISBN: 978-3-96258-109-1
300 Pages, Softcover/Flaps, English

Patricia Paweletz
Tracing the Past in the Present – *En Route to Gaby Glückselig in New York*
ISBN: 978-3-96258-169-5
180 Pages, Non-Fiction, English

YoYo
One Man's Decision to Become a Tree
ISBN: 978-3-96258-136-7
268 Pages, Four Novellas, Softcover/Flaps, English

Rüdiger Görner
The Marble Song
ISBN: 978-3-96258-079-7
280 Pages, Softcover/Flaps, English

Sibylle Prinzessin v. Preussen, Friedrich Wilhelm Prinz v. Preussen
The King's Love – *Frederick the Great, His Gentle Dogs and Other Passions*
ISBN: 978-3-96258-047-6
Translation: Dennis McCort
160 Pages, Biography, Softcover/Flaps, English

Mitya New
Beyond Mount Kailash
ISBN: 978-3-96258-210-4
320 Pages, Novel, English

Sophia Alexandra
Summer on the Subway
ISBN: 978-3-96258-152-7
118 Pages, Poetry, English

Kyricacos Efthymiou
The Red Horse – *Eighteen Short Stories*
ISBN: 978-3-96258-237-1
70 Pages, Poetry, Hardcover, English

Michael Hampe
The Wilderness. The Soul. Nothingness *About the Real Life*
ISBN: 978-3-96258-150-3
390 Pages, Phil. Novel, English

Peter Wortsman
Talking in Tongues – *Essays on Language and Literature*
ISBN: 978-3-96258-233-3
200 Pages, Essays, Softcover/flaps, English

John Berger
garden on my cheek
ISBN: 978-3-941524-77-4
Paintings by Liane Birnberg
60 Pages, Poetry/Art, Softcover/Flaps, English

Michael Hannon
Between Nothing and Nothing at All – *Zwischen Nichts und überhaupt Nichts*
ISBN: 978-3-96258-236-4
90 Pages, Poetry, Hardcover, with images by William T. Wiley
English / German, German translation.: Mitch Cohen, Wolfgang Heyder

Jill Conner, born in the Pacific Northwest, has studied German and Art History in Seattle at the University of Washington and New York at the State University of New York in Stony Brook. She is a descendant of German immigrants who moved to the American Midwest in 1881. As an art critic and curator of emerging contemporary art, she has been inspired by the role of culture as outlined by Norbert Elias and practiced by artists in early 20th-century Berlin. Through the life and work of Max Beckmann, she has examined the ambiguity of culture along with gaps that have emerged from cultural transfer, creating both loss and displacement of a shared cultural memory.